Dark Psychology for Beginners

What are the Secrets of Mind
Manipulation and Control?

Tony Brain

"One does not become enlightened by imagining figures of light, but by making the darkness conscious."

Carl Jung (1875-1961).

Table of Contents

Introduction

It is generally known that knowledge is power. Having said that, possessing human psychology knowledge should be equated to having superpowers. Psychology is the scientific study of the mind of human and how it functions. Psychology covers a wide range of areas including crime to religion, finance, advertising, love, hate, selling and marketing. If you are able to understand the principles of psychology, you have a key to human influence. This is something that is possessed by few people.

To gain psychological knowledge is usually not an easy task as many may think. Just like many of the hidden treasures of man, psychological knowledge is engraved deeply in journals and books. This is of course away from the public's reach. To access this information and make it useful, you may need to go through many journals and books in order to get useful content and separate it from the one that is not useful.

The process of separating has been accomplished. You have access to the finest information which has psychology's most powerful philosophies. All you just need to do is to show your interest in learning, reflecting and practically applying the knowledge you get from this book.

Throughout this book, you will get an insight of the hidden mystery of the world that is understood by only a few people. This is what is referred to as dark psychology. The most powerful influencers use the principles outlined in this book in their journey to being the people they were.

You will know how the principles of the dark of dark psychology are applied. This is of course after getting to know the principles.

Thank you for choosing this book. Enjoy reading!!

Chapter 1: What is the Dark Psychology Story?

Knowing about something that can be used against you gives you agency in those moments when wielding said knowledge can make or break your life. Much like history, your life is probably full of moments where having some insight into dark psychology could have dramatically changed the complexion of your life. There are several good reasons for one to learn about dark psychology. Dark psychology could best be described as a study of the human condition in which it becomes normative for people to pray upon others out of criminal and or deviant desires. Often these desires lack specific purpose and are based primarily on basic instinctual desires. Each human has the potential and capacity to victimize other humans, as well as other living creatures, but most of us keep these desires suppressed in order to function successfully in society. Those of us who do not sublimate these dark tendencies are typically representative of the "dark triad": psychopathy, sociopathy, and Machiavellianism, or other mental disorders/psychological disturbances. In this way, dark psychology focuses primarily on the underpinnings (i.e., the thoughts, processing systems, feelings, and behaviors) that are found below the more predatory aspects of our nature, the same ones that go most vigorously against the grain of modern thought concerning human behavior. In this field, we tend to assume that these more abusive, criminal, and deviant behaviors are purposive most of the time, though there are instances in which they seem to have no teleological underpinnings.

Most people assume that they understand the darker aspects of human nature. They imagine they would be able to see manipulators if they met them and know exactly what to do to keep themselves from being taken advantage of. Most people are wrong.

Evil will not wear a mask that makes it easy to identify. In fact, it will do quite the opposite. It will blend in and gain the target's trust before turning on them and victimizing them. The victim will often realize what's going on when it is already too late for them to do anything about it.

The devil himself is known for taking the ideal form or even appearing as an angel of light. Users of dark psychology are no different. They are master shapeshifters that will take whatever form is necessary to snare their prey. Disguise and deception come naturally to them. So what does one do then?

The best place to start is by educating yourself on their methods. One does not have to use any of them, but they do have to learn enough so they can at least identify the threat when it is present. That is the first step to solving any problem.

The first thing most people don't realize is those dark personality traits are a part of all of us. As such, we all use them to some degree in our daily lives. People around us may even use them on us in ways that are not harmful to us, not realizing what they are doing. Sometimes they may even use them for our own good. Think of mothers telling their kids false facts to get them to eat their vegetables, or trying to trick a drug addicted loved one to go to a place where they'll find their loved ones waiting to ambush them with an intervention.

Well, this chapter will give you some of the examples that you are most likely to meet throughout your life and highlight many of the tricks they might use on you. It leaves out a lot of the more benign examples of the tricks of dark psychology and tells you of the times when there may be high stakes and you cannot afford to be manipulated or blindsided. These can be moments where someone tries to get you to spend more money than you had intended to, or act in a way that may set you down a path that could be disastrous for you.

Principle

Wrongdoing, as Socrates asserts, is doing that harms others. Not only does this harm others, but Socrates also thought that it harms our own souls, as many modern people would agree. Dark psychologists allow that some of us do wrong onto others for no greater purposes. Their ends never justify their means because there are simply no ends to be found. This capability (and perhaps even proclivity) for harm within cause or purposiveness can be found within all of us. The field of dark psychology assumes justifiably that these irrational desires to harm within us are incredibly complex and hard to understand.

Whether wrongdoing is purposive or even intentional, and whether it is done out of want of money, retaliation, or power, the most destructive force behind wrongdoing is aggression. Aggression is likely the single biggest adversary of prosocial relations, and it should not be confused with assertiveness. Aggression is any verbal and or physical behavior that is meant to harm or destroy. This aim is what differentiates it from other classes of behaviors that bring harm or destruction with no aims.

Biologically, there are certain genetic markers that are more indicative of aggression than others. Neurologically, it is the amygdala that controls most aggressive behavioral patterns. For this reason, people with enlarged and deformed amygdala typically commit violent acts at higher rates. As far as hormones are concerned, it is usually those people (primarily young men) with higher levels of testosterone and lower levels of serotonin who tend to be the most violent. The most aggressive people within societies are typically ones who have been put through something of a loop: their testosterone levels rise and cause them to become aggressive, which in turn begets higher levels of testosterone and even more aggression. In this way, some of the most dangerous people the world has to offer are created. Drugs and foods that increase serotonin and decrease testosterone levels are typically the best options for decreasing overall levels of aggression.

The most common cause of aggression is a failure or being stopped short of a goal. Studies indicate that those who have been made miserable by such unfortunate events usually make others around them more miserable as well. In these unpleasant instances, we naturally become frustrated, which begets our being angered, and once we are angered, we can easily become aggressive if given a cue. Some of the most common stimuli that can cue aggressive behaviors are personal insults (perhaps the most common), cigarette smoke, foul odors, and hot temperatures. Ostracism is another common cause of aggression, causing some of the same neurological phenomena as physical pain does.

Chapter 2: The dark core of personality/Dark Factor of Personality

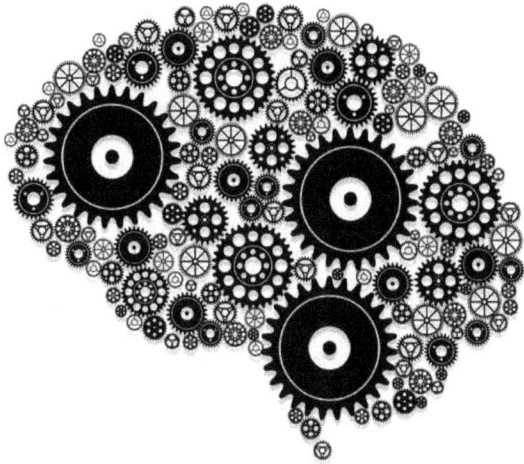

We seem to concentrate too much on the easier side the of human psychology. Whether those followers of the "positive psychology" movement or not, we often tend to have difficulty seeing the value in the more rank underbelly of human psychology, the dark side. This happens to our detriment though, as it is the more bothersome aspects of our nature that tend to enlighten us more than the personas that people put on. Here we will delve into the darker traits of human psychology, the ones that all contain one overarching trait more destructive than any others: callousness or a lack of empathy for others. Those who have these traits are very diverse, but they all share the potential to harm others due to their inability to empathize.

The first of these traits, and perhaps the most common is narcissism. We all display this negative trait at one point or another, so it is usually best to reserve judgment when others come across as narcissistic upon first glance. Narcissists often disregard the thoughts and feelings of others and take advantage of people in order to get what they want. Witnessing other people getting attention and admiration frustrates them, as they believe that they are entitled to these things above others. This trait, like any other, exists on a spectrum within people, with the most pretentious of us at the top and the ones with least self-efficacy at the bottom.

Although all of us experience narcissistic traits in varying degrees, in around 1% of the population these traits can take on a more severe, pathological form in which the person gains an unrealistic perception of his or her own abilities and is in constant need of attention and admiration. This anthologized form of narcissism is called narcissistic personality disorder.

Narcissistic supply is a sort of admiration, sustenance, or interpersonal support drawn by a narcissist out of his or her environment. This supply can easily become essential to the maintenance of the narcissist's self-esteem if it is never kept from him or her. For this reason, narcissists tend to seek out those who will admire them irrationally and there is very little chance that will stop a narcissist once he or she has found some sort of relationship in which there are unjustified resources allocated interpersonally. This need for the admiration or attention of codependents is considered pathological because it does not take into account the feeling, thoughts, and or needs of the other people involved. The narcissist only considers his or her supply and is never focused on what is actually going on with those other people involved.

Narcissistic injury is something seen as a danger to the so called narcissist's self-esteem. Other terms interchangeable with this one are a narcissistic blow, narcissistic scar, and narcissistic wound. What all of these have in common, however, is what they are met with narcissistic rage. Narcissistic rage is known as a common reaction to any form of narcissistic injury. Now this rage (like any other sort of rage) exists within a continuum, ranging from mild remoteness to harsher expressions of annoyance and frustration, and finally to intense emotional outbursts, sometimes including violent attacks.

Narcissistic rage can manifest itself in many other ways as well. These include depressive, paranoid delusion, and catatonic episodes. It is also widely held that most narcissists have two major types of rage. Mainly the first of type is the rage constantly directed at one or more other people, while the second type is constantly directed at the self. Narcissistic rage is not necessarily troublesome in its severity, as its severity exists on a similar spectrum as does "normal" rage, but becomes more problematic when considering that it is inherently pathological.

The narcissistic defense is any process whereby the idealized self portrait of the narcissist is preserved, while any of its actual limitations are denied. In other words, this type of defense is found when the narcissist is trying to preserve his or her own self-image more so than trying to ascertain the truth about the self. These defenses tend to be very rigid, as the narcissist anchors as much as possible to the most self-flattering narratives imaginable. Most narcissists actually do experience feelings of guilt or shame (both conscious and unconscious) quite often, and one of the most common methods by which they alleviate these negative feelings is by putting up such defenses. Pathological narcissism has to find psychological shortcuts in order to survive throughout greater self-realization, and narcissistic defense is likely the most common of these shortcuts.

The original definition of narcissistic abuse referred more to the abuse committed by narcissistic parents on their children. Typically, this type of abuse consists of the children of narcissists having to give up parts of their own feelings and wants in order to protect their parents' self-esteems. Children who grow up being subjected to this type of abuse often have codependency issues later on in life. Having no knowledge of what constitutes a normal relationship, they tend to be unable to recognize who it is who they will be better off with and who to avoid. It is common that they will formulate further relationships with more narcissists who have similar pathologies to those of their parents.

In more recent years this term has been more widely applied to abuse within relationships among adults. Adult narcissists are about as likely to abuse other adults as they are to abuse children. These abusive relationships typically do not last as long due to the fact that adult victims usually have much more mobility to get out of the relationships than do child victims.

The next dark trait is Machiavellianism. This term can be applied to both the political philosophy of Niccolò Machiavelli and a manipulative personality trait. Here only the later usage will apply. This trait is most commonly characterized by a deceitful personality style, a pathological focus on personal gain and self-interest, an overall deficiency of empathy, and a blatant disregard for morality.

One of the most troubling aspects of Machiavellians is their overall lack of emotion. This often leads them to be influenced very little by "conventional" modes of morality and to subsequently manipulate and deceive others without remorse in order to meet their own personal needs. This trait is measured in units called machs by psychologists. People with higher levels of machs are shown to agree more with statements such as "never tell others your reasoning unless it benefits you to do so", and less with statements such as "people are generally good", "there is never an excuse to lie to others", or "the most successful among us lead moral lives". Typically, males score higher levels of machs than do females.

Machiavellians are typically rather cold and selfish people who see others mostly as instruments they can use to serve their own interests. The motives that they have in mind at any given point in time, whether they be sexual, social, professional, etc., are often pursued in duplicitous manners, with little to no thought of the wellbeing of the other parties involved in mind. Those with higher levels of machs tend to be motivated more by power, money, and competition than anything else, while those with lower levels of machs tend to focus more on things such as family commitment, self-love, and community building. People with higher levels of machs want to win at any cost, no matter how steep. With these views in mind, we could reasonably argue that people who are more Machiavellian than others are also more bent toward avarice. These people are typically much less motivated by altruistic sentiments and any forms of philanthropy, and instead, spend most of their time in aimless competition and malevolent industry. For these reasons, Machiavellians are usually much less trustworthy and much more self-interested than others.

It is only their outstanding abilities in manipulating others that give Machiavellians the reputation of being an intelligent group of people. In reality, there is no verifiable correlation between machs and IQ scores, but the stereotype of the intelligent Machiavellian shifting his or her way through vast webs of action and coming out with everything in mind persists, nevertheless. Emotional intelligence is, however, not a strong point of most Machiavellians. Higher levels of machs are typically correlated with lower EQ scores. Both emotional recognition and emotional empathy are negatively correlated with Machiavellianism. This trait has also never been shown to be correlated to a more advanced theory of mind. This suggests that Machiavellians are not necessarily better able to understand what others are thinking in social situations, so any abilities in manipulation they might possess are not related to their theory of mind.

Chapter3: Case Studies

It may come as a surprise the different ways that dark psychology appears in real life. There are obvious cases of rampant brutality and the will to overpower others. Then there are the more subtle forms that it can present itself. Anyone and everyone are capable of using dark psychology. All it takes is one bad day, or a string of bad days to change someone. Certain "bad apples" are rotten from the start, and can't do anything to change the fact. Not that these individuals are even willing to admit there is something wrong with them. Or that they may even want to change in the first place. Finally, dark psychology applies to those sad cases where people with mental illness could not get the help that they needed and succumbed to the influence of the dark triad. There is no known cure for psychopathy, but several "treatment" options have emerged in clinical psychology. Personality disorders, in general, have targeted by CBT techniques to some success. Changing the behavior patterns and self-image of a psychopath on a fundamental level is difficult for many reasons. For one, within the dark triad, there is the perfect recipe for disaster consisting of self-importance, narcissism and an inflated ego. In other words, the psychopath doesn't want to be cured, unless if by submitting to the treatment they get something out of it, like avoiding jail time or having a reduced sentence.

Dark psychology is responsible for fringe behavior and is often lumped with criminality. Breaking the law, causing bodily or mental harm to others or to self, always finds its way back to dark psychology. Whether it is the desire to hurt someone, use someone for personal gain, revenge or for some other reason. Mental illness seems to be the exception here but may still result in dark psychological tendencies. Suicide, for example, is thought to be caused by depression and doesn't directly relate to dark psychology.

Case: *Murder of Kayla Rolland*

Dark Psychology Involvement: Patterns of child neglect, possibly resulting in psychopathic tendencies

The story of Kayla Roland is a sad one. Up until the Sandy Hook shooting, she was considered the youngest school shooting victim. She was only six and a first grader going to school near Flint, Michigan. One of her classmates, Dederick Owens, was a problem child early on. He reportedly bullied her on previous occasions and was cruel to other students. His many behavioral problems were noted by the school staff, but little was done to correct them. With his father in jail and his mother being a drug addict, he'd had a tough life. Owens brought a small handgun to school one day and shot and killed Kayla Roland in front of the rest of the class.

At the time, Owens was under the custody of his uncle, who ran a drug operation out of his home.

Owens was exposed at a very young age to adult violence, drug use, and firearms, which no doubt contributed to his behavior. Normally, young children are excused from having psychopathic diagnoses because of their age (and supposed innocence). But Owens showed the classic signs of psychopathy. He routinely followed Kayla around and wanted to be her friend. In one instance, he attempted to kiss her but was rejected. Just moments before shooting her, Owens told her, "I don't like you" and pulled the trigger.

Here the dark triad is apparent in the Machiavellianism behind the shooting. Owens seemed to be dealing with jealously or some other emotion towards Kayla, which resulted in him acquiring a firearm behind everyone's knowledge and shooting her like it was nothing. Coupled with frequent fights with other students and violent behavior, Owns had all the making of a psychopath. Unfortunately, it was the rotten situation in which he grew up that probably fueled his actions. Guns were easily accessible in the house (he found the handgun under some blankets). And the adults around him normalized violent and anti-social behavior, to the point where murdering a classmate didn't seem so bad.

Case: *Jonestown Massacre*

Dark Psychology Involvement: Cult following, brainwash, deceit, covert manipulation

The Jonestown cult was started by Jim Jones, a charismatic man who opened up to his followers as a guru. They called themselves the Peoples Temple and started a new age religious movement. Jones attracted many people, from all walks of life and religious backgrounds. Paramount to his mission was racial equality, social justice and utopianism. Many found in the Peoples Temple what they could not find in other religious followings. The Temple allowed just about anyone to join as long as they believed in Jone's teachings.

Unfortunately, Jones was a con man from the start. He would schedule fundraising and recruiting events by visiting major cities all across the US with a core group of followers. They would all take Greyhound buses to their destination and invite locals to join them for service. During the service members of the Peoples Temple stood in with the local audience, often outnumbering them by a large amount. Then Jones would perform "cures" on stage, calling up selected followers to act the part of somebody being miraculously cured of their afflictions.

Followers were subjected to all sorts of sexual abuse and psychological brainwashing by their leader. Jones didn't allow members to have sex with another partner inside the church unless they were married, and he frequently had sexual relations with whoever he wished. Many of his followers came from broken homes or were children of abuse. He stood out as a father figure, and it was common that a follower called him "Father."

Jonestown was built by followers hands. They were overworked in the sweaty jungles of Guyana, meanwhile given little to eat and slept odd hours. Jones cut off all informational sources, making him the one stop for news about the world. He convinced his followers of terrible things happening in America and of the possibility of a race war. He also made them believe that their commune would be targeted next. Jones organized a little loyalty test, where he had followers drink from a vat of "poison" that really was just a flavored drink. He told them that the armed forces had landed, and were going to kill them anyways. So they drank. Jones then informed them that it had all been a test, and his followers received praise.

Growing ever more delusional, Jones set up the same trick again, only this time lacing the drink with cyanide poison. Many followers believed it was a test again, but Jones talked about a "revolutionary suicide" on the loudspeakers. Others resisted and had the poison administered by force by Jone's armed personnel. Of those who willingly took the drink, had the poison injected, or thought that it was a test, some 900 died including 300 children.

Case: *Islamic Radicalization*

Dark Psychology Involvement: Brainwash, deceit, covert manipulation

Islamic terrorists are increasingly being radicalized by local terrorist cells abroad. Many of the terrorist attacks in recent years where perpetrated by young men who had an implanted ideology. This can either happen in their home country before leaving or in the host country by local groups. Radicalization works best with younger individuals, usually migrants or refugees who are at odds with the major population. They feel alienated and are either unwilling to assimilate to the new culture or find it incredibly hard to do so.

They then get singled out by religious leaders or terrorist cells who want to recruit them. The usual tools of dark psychological attacks commence. First, the individual is alienated or isolated in the style of the Jonestown victims and fed lies about the people they are ordered to attack. They are told that what they are doing is good and that they will be rewarded for it. Or that by becoming a martyr, they are fighting for the greater good.

Radicalization can happen to just about anyone, given the right toolset and or circumstances. When dark psychology isn't enough, brute force can help turn the tides. That is what happened in 2014 when 148 Kurdish boys and teens were kidnapped by ISIL in Syria. Historical, Kurds and Sunni ISIL fighters do not like each other. Kurdish forces have constant clashes with the terrorist group. But through a blend of propaganda, torture and violence, the Kurdish boys came to accept the teachings of ISIL as true. They believed that their mission was the righteous one, despite being against their own ethnic group.

Case: *Kidnapping and Abuse of Colleen Stan*

Dark Psychology Involvement: abuse, covert manipulation, deceit, kidnap

Colleen was only 20 when she tried hitching a ride from her home in Eugene, Oregon to a friend's house who lived in northern California. A man named Cameron Hooker picked her up. At first appearances, Hooker seemed like a decent person. He was riding with his wife and infant baby in the front. But after they stopped at a gas station, Hooker veered off the highway and put a knife to Stan's throat.

What ensued was a horrific period of seven years where Colleen was subjected to sex slavery and false imprisonment in a coffin-like box. It was reported that she was only allowed a few hours outside of the box daily, was maltreated and used to do Hooker's bidding. During this time Colleen was also being brainwashed by Hooker, who broke her down emotionally and referred to her only as "K." Hooker was to be addressed as "master" at all times. Colleen was told a fantastic story about an underground organization that would kill her family if she ever tried to escape or resist. And even when Colleen could have escaped or run to the authorities in that seven-year period, she refused to do so. On one occasion, even being allowed to visit her family, Colleen presented Hooker as her boyfriend and said nothing more about it.

There is reason to believe that Hooker was also using dark psychological attacks against his wife, Janice. Janice allowed the abuse to go on because in a way, it absolved her from her previous position as Hooker's sex slave. It is perhaps the main reason why Janice allowed the relationship with the kidnapped girl to go on.

Dark Psychology Spectrum

Common to all these examples is a combination of dark psychology and violence. In the real world, these are extreme and isolated instances of people using dark psychology against others. One is less likely to encounter such extremes in their daily life, but they do outline the underline power, and what may ultimately result from when using dark psychology. Minor interference with dark psychology like trying to get someone fired in the workplace will rarely balloon to criminal offenses.

There is a spectrum between the purely mental and purely violent means to manipulate someone. Kidnapping and then using brainwashing to control the victim lean towards the violent side. This book does not cover the physical side of dark psychology, nor does it touch on instances of physical torture. These are tried and tested methods for breaking someone psychologically but only using physical force. They are routinely used by armed forces against enemies.

Psychopaths may tend towards the violent side if they believe it will get them what they want. Others who dabble with dark psychology, whether intentionally or not, are iffy about crossing the physical violence boundary. And for a good reason, too. Violence is readily accepted as a criminal offense in varying degrees. It also brings up obvious ethical considerations. Such considerations are easier to excuse or ignore if the manipulation is purely non-physical. Though even the ethics of any dark psychological attack are noteworthy, it is up to the attacker whether they think using them is justified.

In the end, it will be up to the court system to decide if such things are ethical. Some techniques on the dark psychology spectrum like blackmail are punishable by law. Most of the time, somebody using dark psychology for bad will be charged under a different, more pressing charge like fraud, extortion, or workplace harassment. In general, any given dark psychology attack is not in and of itself considered a crime.

Key Points

> ➤ People who show characteristics that belong to the dark triad are more likely to use dark psychology to manipulate others

- Using dark psychology does not automatically make someone a psychopath or put them under a dark triad classification
- The same underlying techniques that make dark psychology possible can also be used for good
- Dark psychology does not necessarily constitute a crime but may implicate other criminal behavior
- Case studies into who uses dark psychology and why tend to be extreme or sensational in nature. They are what you typically hear on the news. What is more threatening is the type of manipulation you don't hear about. Things that happen daily in relationships, companies, and out on the streets.

Action Items

1.   At some point in your life, you will have to interact with a psychopath. Making up 1% of the population, this much is inevitable. If you live in a city of at least one million, that means there are around 100,000 of these individuals walking around. Some may have a narcissist in their daily lives or somebody who is always scheming. Examine your close and distant relationships for any signs of the dark triad. Is there somebody who is egotistical, overly cruel, or remorseless? If so, do you believe you are currently or have ever been under a dark psychological attack by them?

2.   Documentaries, interviews, and news reports are a treasure trove of dark psychology evidence. Many victims talk about how their captors took away their sense of identity little by little and then started to manipulate them. There is much to learn from these lucky survivors who made it out alive. Pick any of the case studies

above or find your own, and watch a few of the first-hand material found online. Who were the people who fell to cults, and why did they do it? How did the scenario affect their lives going forward?

Chapter4: Manipulation

Dark Psychology is all about manipulation. That's its essence. Every Dark Personality, every Dark Trait, almost every Dark Tactic has at its root manipulation.

Manipulation is all around us—through advertising, marketing, from our parents, our supervisors, our lovers, the layout of our local mall. It so completely is a part of our lives we hardly notice it. So when a Psychopath, a Machiavellian approaches us with a request, an ask, a piece of information, no wonder we're not always aware that they're after something. Us, most likely. Or something we have—money, power, our bodies. And we all do it, sometimes it's just a white lie, sometimes flattery, sometimes complete subterfuge. For those of the Dark Triad, however, manipulation is a way of life. They are, to be ungentle about it, predators. And we are their prey.

But let's also be clear about the difference between manipulation and influence. (Influence, it could be argued—that's really what's all around us, via ads and the internet and from our friends and teachers. And subliminal influencing, via subliminal messages, those are definitely covert and underhanded, but used less by individual Dark

Personalities and more by governments, advertising, TV, music, and movies—as popularized and demonized in Vance Packard's 1957 classic expose, The Hidden Persuaders, in which Packard claimed that those playing the advertising role used Americans' unconscious needs so that they would buy items they did not desire or even need. Manipulative, for sure. Pathological, no.)

So. The Difference between manipulation and influence. Manipulation often causes confusion, anxiety, depression, and powerlessness. It's unpleasant, it's demeaning. Manipulative relationships are destructive. Manipulators do not care what happens to their targets. Manipulators only want what they want—and the consequences are damned.

People who seek to influence others, they have a positive intent. Their self-esteem does not depend on the actions of the person they are seeking to influence. Influence also involves open and direct communication. The influencer behaves with clarity and transparency and a clear goal, which is usually to the benefit of both parties, if not entirely for the benefit of the person being influenced. And the person being influenced is not just allowed to think for themselves, they're often encouraged to think for themselves and to make their own decisions.

Manipulators lie. They manipulate covertly, indirectly, underhandedly. They feel justified, entitled, rightful to treat others however they choose. Manipulators also see the world in zero-sum terms. Play or get played. Eat or be eaten. The world to them is black and white. For them, a relationship is a power struggle, a connection but one on unequal terms. Terms in their favor, terms they control. Ultimately, they do not trust others—because they know that they themselves are not trustworthy.

Before I begin my attack, I must first become acquainted with her and her whole mental state.

Søren Kierkegaard, The Seducer's Diary

What sort of targets, then, do Manipulators prey on? Do they have a particular type? They do: someone with issues. Unresolved issues. Issues Manipulators can sniff out, then exploit. People struggling with low self-esteem, a good number are naïve, very easy to please, too eager to please, unassertive, lacking in confidence—these are the most vulnerable. People with certain weaknesses like the ones below. If any of these strike a chord, if you have any of these tendencies, any of these behaviors, work on them. Don't try to hide them or hope a Manipulator won't detect them. Work on them. They are:

An unhealthy need to please: The target, fearful of rejection, disapproval, abandonment—of introducing the slightest dose of reality into the relationship—keeps everything as pleasant as possible.

Sometimes the urge of feeling the need to earn that very approval and acceptance from other people: Sometimes corresponds to a lack of confidence in one's own judgments—especially of others. Especially when it comes to Manipulators—who put on a very convincing front but to a target, often just feel off. But without a solid sense of self, the target yields to others. This need for approval can then cloud one's trust in oneself, in one's visceral reaction to a Manipulator.

Cannot say No!: Or just No, thank you. A lack of assertiveness, especially, again, when it comes to one's feelings or one's own needs or wants.

Soft personal boundaries: A murky sense of who you are. Your identity rests too much in others and you tend to merge or lose yourself in another person's boundaries. A person just one step up from soft, who has spongy boundaries is, according to Old Dominion professor by the name Nina Brown, known as an author of Coping With Infuriating, Critical People—Call them Destructive Narcissistic Pattern, Mean, someone with soft and rigid boundaries. People with soft boundaries are not sure of who to open up to and who to keep out.

Low self-reliance: You tend to cling to others and rely on them and can even see them as superior or more powerful. You're emotionally dependent, submissive.

Fear of negative emotions: You cannot express anger, frustration, or disapproval. What Harriet B. Braiker, author of The Disease To Please, calls "emotophobia."

The feeling that an individual doesn't feel in control and that more so everything is someone else's fault: If the situation of being in the drivers seat is the degree to which an individual will believe they have the power of the resulting outcome of events in the pattern of their lives, people with an external locus of control blame (or thank) outside factors for what happens in their lives.

And two others: the overly conscientious—targets who are ever willing to provide the Manipulator the satisfaction of the benefit of the doubt—more so the over-intellectualizer—the target who is intent on figuring out why it is the Manipulator continues to do the things they do, all the while staying with the Manipulator rather than leaving.

Whether or not you are on this list, being manipulated is not your fault. Manipulators know what they're doing. They are in control. The manipulated, though, until they see it, they have little idea what's going on. Even so, it is still up to the target of the Manipulator to put up boundaries. That is not victim blaming, it's just how it is. The Manipulator will not stop until their target puts a stop to their behavior. Otherwise, there's no incentive. Things are working out great for them; they're getting exactly what they want. Why stop? The solution: Stop rewarding their tactics. Manipulation exists because it works.

The techniques of manipulation are many—and seemingly endless. Here are some—some of the ones used most often by Dark Personality types.

Love Bombing (aka Love Flooding): Unlike the display of a healthy romantic level of interest, Love Bombing happens too fast and comes on way too strong. The Manipulator immediately want to spend every moment with you; they're madly in love with you right there at the bar, in the middle of happy hour. According to Michael Pace, author of Dark Psychology, Mind Games, And Other Tricks Of The Trade including Brainwashing, Love bombing has almost nothing to do with love. It's all a ruse—the early stage of the Manipulator readying his victim.

Positive Reinforcement: After the Love Bombing comes positive reinforcement, which comes in many forms, from outright praise and superficial charm straight to superficial sympathy as they say (crocodile tears) and exceedingly apologizing. As Dark Psychology author Michael Pace explains it, this comes soon after the Love Bombing. Only it's hardly at all positive. Instead, the Manipulator has stopped Love Bombing altogether and replaced it with . . . crickets. For instance, the target must wear a certain dress the Manipulator gave them before the Manipulator will give them a kiss. The target has no idea that the kiss comes not from the Manipulator's desire for her, it's because he coerced her into doing what he wanted.

Negative Reinforcement: Even though that behavior is not deliberate, the Manipulator uses negative reinforcement to get you, the target, to adopt to his wishes, his demands—no matter how unreasonable.

Love Denial/Love Withdrawal: First he Giveth, then he Taketh away. After all that love, the Manipulator lets the target know just who's boss by withdrawing all that love and attention and affection. If the Manipulator doesn't out-and-out leave, their love its quality, its frequency, its expression morphs into something altogether . . . different. As if you have less value than the day before they professed their undying love for you.

Diversion: The Manipulator won't give you a clear and straight answer, even to questions that need a No or Yes answer, and instead often drives the conversation to some another topic.

Evasion: Just like Diversion but now the Manipulator gives unclear, rambling, and irrelevant responses—weasel words—words or even statements that are seemingly intentional when it comes to misleading or ambiguous. Shaming is and can be subtle to a disappointed look, a tone of voice, a mean glance—and mostly they are hugely effective at bringing that very sense or thought of inadequacy in the given target.

Vilifying the Victim: This is mostly used by the Manipulator as another way of getting over their guilt over some wrongdoing they've committed, this is when and how the Manipulator depicts someone else in the worst possible light in order to justify their own behaviors. It's a rather ingenious way of creating confusion about who the real target is. They falsely blame others to shirk free of any responsibility or accountability for their actions. I slept with your best friend but you pushed me into it. Worse, if the target defends themselves or their position, the Manipulator, in response, falsely accuses the target as being the abuser.

Projecting Blame (Blaming Others): Manipulators are so effective because unless they work in such subtle, hard-to-detect, nearly impossible to explain ways. Projecting blame, where the Manipulator scapegoats the target, is particularly insidious. A combination of misdirection and blame-shifting, the Manipulator casts their flaws and feelings onto the target: "I was late for an important meeting because you said I had to pick up the kids." Projecting blame is repeatedly a way of psychological plus emotional manipulations. Manipulators often do lie about lying, to continuously manipulate and re-manipulate the original, the less believable kind of a story into a realistically "more acceptable" that the target will definitely believe to be the truth. Another tactic is visualizing lies to being the truth. Manipulators often love to point accusing figures falsely to accuse theire target as if they deserve to be treated in that manner. Manipulators will often point solidly and claim that their target is crazy or even abusive, (See Feigning, below.)

Moving the Goalposts: You might think you know where you stand with a Manipulator, but if they are constantly moving the goalposts in order to confuse you, then it's likely you're dealing with a predator. The ground is always shifting. One day the Manipulator tells you to leave the lights on, the next day he berates you for not having turned the lights off.

Gaslighting: A nefarious tactic, akin to brainwashing. The Manipulator makes the target to believe and to doubt themself, and eventually lose her very own thought and sense of perception, talk of self-worth and most of all identity. The Manipulator: C'mon. I never told you that. Or: You're being paranoid. Or: Why are you making such a big deal out of this?

Feigning Innocence/Ignorance: The Manipulator, playing the innocence card, draws an illustration to suggest that every harm done was not intentional or in other words what they are accused of never happened. The target feels like a false accuser, a perpetrator, and often questions their judgment and their sanity.

Feigning Confusion: Manipulator pretend to be dumb, making it look as if they do not have an idea of what the target is actually talking about or even pretend they are confused and not focused about an important issue being brought to their knowledge. You even find the Manipulator having to intentionally confuse the target to purposely make the target doubt their own sense of the accuracy of their perception, mostly to point out the key elements the Manipulator indeed intentionally included just there is a reason to doubt.

Brandishing Anger: Manipulator brings anger to play, the intensity of emotional, and aggressiveness to shock and make the target panic resulting into submission. In this case you find that the Manipulator is actually not angry, this is just a false act.The aggressiveness "anger" is mostly and highly effective as a way in which the Manipulator uses to avoid telling what is actually the truth at those inconvenient moments and/or circumstances; the target—scared, uncertain if the anger is genuine or not—becomes more focused on the anger instead of either the original topic or the tactics of manipulation.

Bandwagon Effect: The Manipulator uses their bag of tricks by pretending to comfort the target to actually submit by making it seem like they are claiming whether it's true or false that other people are doing it, so you can too. It mostly surfaces in situations where the Manipulator does always try to influence their target into trying different things like for example sexual acts or drugs.

In the case of such scenarios or behaviors hits a nerve, there's manipulation going on. And the only real way to stop the manipulation from continuing is to stop falling into the manipulation. Don't fool yourself into thinking that if the Manipulator knew better they would treat you better. The more victimized you feel, the less you will feel able to powerful over yourself or your life. As you become more diminished, you to change the manipulator, focus on changing you and your behavior.

Chapter5:   NLP   (Neuro-Linguistic Programming)

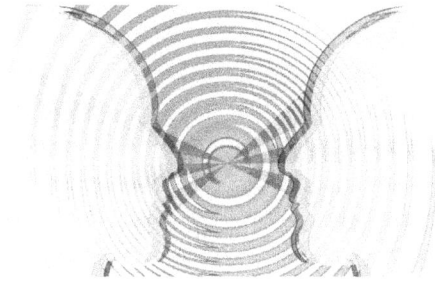

What is hypnosis?

This is just the way that people may use hypnosis to influence people around them without their knowledge. This can be thought of as 'covert hypnosis'. It may not always be as hard to detect and malevolent as most people might think. However, its power and widespread influence should never be underestimated.

This involves avoiding the critical thinking portions of the brain and embedding ideas in the deeper parts of the mind that we don't consciously control. While most people will innocently use a lot of these techniques without realizing it, there are those who know exactly what they are doing and intentionally using them on unsuspecting people.

Who is most likely to use it on you?

We come across covert hypnosis all the time without realizing it. While it can't be used to brainwash and mind-control people the way you see on stage or in the movies, it's still a powerful tool for gaining the compliance of people around you.

One will come across it most often in everyday life when advertisers want to get you to buy something. They want your money, not your consent. To this end, they research ways to get you to comply and give them your money without asking questions.

Other people in power who want unquestioned followers will use these techniques as well, like televangelists and politicians.

Tactics

Dominate the subject's attention

The reason you are most likely to see hypnotism used on you while you watch television or surf the web is because that is when you are fully engrossed in what you are doing and are in an attentive state of mind that leaves you highly suggestible.

When someone has your full attention to the point where time seems to fly and everything else seems to matter a bit less is when they have the most power over you. This is when you're more likely to register the things they say on a deeper level than you usually do, to the point of not thinking critically about what they were saying.

Think of the last time you were enjoying a book or conversation to the point where time flew by you.

How much time do you think you spent engaging your critical mind to question what was going on and fact check?

Engage imagination

Taking someone on an imaginative journey to some special place in their minds where they are more likely to feel safe is where they are more likely to be open to influence and suggestion. You'll often find hypnotherapists and other types of hypnotists using a method that applies to this principle.

This is because the imagination is a powerful tool. If you can get someone to picture themselves doing something and not regretting it for any reason, then you open them up to a new world where a new option is open to them. As long as the target feels safe and in control then they won't even realize their imagination is being used against them.

Soft commands

This is a great way to bypass the critical part of the brain that registers things like right and wrong. This is more likely to work because trying to give a hard command like, "you will lose weight" is less likely to activate any resistance from the critical part of the brain. You will have better chances with a soft command like, "how jealous will your ex be once you've lost weight?"

The brain often doesn't even register this as a command and will focus on the part it finds the most appealing. Just listen to commands that require you to do something without actually asking your consent about whether you want to do said something. This makes you think the idea was all yours when it was actually placed there by someone else.

Linking presupposition

This one is a bit trickier to pull off than one would expect as it requires more finesse than most people are willing to practice to muster. It involves a lot of different elements and can have a lot of moving parts, but can be useful to learn to spot or even use.

Linking presupposition involves asking someone to do something that seems to line up with what they were going to do anyway. Think of someone suggesting you add some special package on a car you're buying even though you may not need it. Sounds familiar right? That's because it is.

When done right, it can make people take on more than they had initially intended. One simply needs to get someone to imagine that taking that small extra step won't do any harm when they were already headed in that direction anyway.

Reality stacking

You will often find politicians and seducers doing this. It involves getting people emotional about things they agree with and then slotting their own agendas in there as if it was a natural extension of the discussion that was missing until just then.

Once you have someone feeling relaxed in the thought that they understand where you're coming from and then aligning yourself with the ideas they carried all along then they will be more likely to see you or your suggestion linking to their ideas as plausible and maybe even natural. You will often hear advertisers doing something similar, especially when advertising for a pharmaceutical company.

The realities don't actually have to have that strong a link to begin with. Just get people saying 'yes' enough times and they will want to keep saying it because it continues a trend. Trends are easier to follow than they are to break, so they'll likely just keep going with it.

Strongly descriptive language

This isn't inherently bad. It's often used by a lot of people when they are trying to tell a really good story. However, there are those who know that the minds love of descriptive knowledge is the quickest path past their logical brain and right to their emotional brain.

It is common for parents to use this language to explain tricky concepts to children since it is easier to understand. On the other hand, it can also be used by manipulators (like lawyers and dark seducers) to get people to believe them without asking too many questions.

Answering a question or telling a story with as much descriptive language as possible will make someone think that they are being told the truth and want to follow the emotional content of the story more than the intellectual content. This is the power of painting word pictures in people's' minds.

Hidden suggestion

The tactic of hiding a suggestion relies on subtle plays on words that might register as a slip of the tongue or the target simply mishearing what was being said. This is more of a one-on-one trick than anything else and requires you to pay attention in case it isn't as innocent as one may think.

The hidden suggestion involves sliding a suggestion in the place of something that sounds very similar. Almost mumbling words like 'die' in the place of words like 'dine' will slowly ingrain the idea of death in someone's mind. It doesn't have to be the said every time, but enough times that it starts to settle in the victim's mind.

Catching someone doing this will not always be easy as they can turn the tables on you and say that they aren't saying it and you must actually have it on your mind if you keep hearing it.

Tone/language mimicry

A dark hypnotist can, in a one-on-one setting, listen out for some of the words a target uses the most when they are feeling a certain way. They can then use them against them when they are trying to invoke certain emotions to lower their opponent's guard and make them more compliant.

This can also be done with vocal tone. If someone memorizes how your voice changes when you say certain things then they can mimic that tone of voice to make people gradually open up to wanting to listen to them when they say particular things in that specific tone.

The ideas said in those moments will feel more like they come from the mind of the target more than they do from the mouth of the manipulator.

Environmental stimulus

A manipulator can open a target to being more agreeable by making it a point to associate certain places with certain emotions. For example, they can give you a small gift every time you pass a certain place until your mind comes to expect it. Once your mind has linked that place with receiving a gift then you are more likely to take on a receptive attitude when you are near that place.

It can also be used to put things in a certain environment that trigger unpleasant emotions. They may put certain things, like images of snakes, in the background of places they want you to feel fear in. Once they have the feelings triggered, they can use the emotional state they induced to slowly change your perception of certain things.

Engage all the senses

Hypnosis works well when it engages as many senses as possible. Once the mind is too busy being engaged on multiple levels, then it starts to lose the ability to focus on detecting threats. Your full attention needs to be where the hypnotist needs it to be.

So when they use words to engage your senses, then your mind becomes too preoccupied to think too hard on things like right and wrong. The heightened state of awareness pointed in another direction makes it easier to subtly plant ideas into the mind of an unsuspecting target.

It relies on the same fundamental principles that are used in magic tricks, pick-pocketing and even martial arts. It's the old story of the magic trick not being where you're looking.

NLP

NLP, which is short for Neuro-Linguistic Programming, is a practice that studies how people map out the world around them in their minds. It also studies how to read these maps people make in their minds and remap them where and when it is necessary. The people who put these kinds of ideas and techniques together were Richard Bandler and John Grinder back in 1975.

While it may use a lot of techniques found in hypnosis, it is important to note that NLP is not hypnosis. It merely draws on the scientific elements of hypnosis, along with many other practices, in an attempt to create a structured way to gain power over 'the voices on their heads' and change their lives.

NLP is widely used by many professionals in high-pressure jobs as well as life coaches in order to get the best out of one's mind in the least harmful ways possible. Many successful people who have used (or still use) NLP will attest to the power of reprogramming one's thoughts and using the mind as a tool to better oneself. However, NLP can also have a very dark side.

Because of the power of self-awareness can create in one's own mind to control themselves, it can also give dark personalities the power to control others. This becomes possible when you realize that the tactics used in NLP can covertly be used on other people once a person becomes adept enough at using them.

State Calibration

State calibration is when one pays very close attention to the person, or people, they are interacting with. They look for the smallest changes in body language. Being well versed in how to read moods and emotions through facial expressions and body language, a person will use this information to change their own state in a way that keeps the other person under their influence.

This touches on the subject of mirroring and works best while still building rapport and deepening the bond one has with a target. Having enough understanding of how thoughts and feelings affect body language can help a neuro-linguistic programmer who knows what they are doing to keep matching or complimenting a person's moods with their own.

Using state calibration well can be a powerful way to build a deep bond with someone and get them in a more trusting mood. Since most people only partially give their attention to people, a target may register this deep reading as the persuader being interested in them to the point of giving them their full attention. People are more likely to like people they are convinced likes them.

On top of building rapport, knowing how to analyze like this may help better detect how someone feels about you, someone else or even themselves. It can also help tell if someone is being deceitful as the moods of most people will change very slightly when they lie.

Anchoring

This is a technique that draws directly from hypnosis. It involves linking a certain emotion to a specific gesture, pose, motion, object, etc. It can be used on oneself or their opponent. It does not have to be negative, but one will see how it can take on darker tones when used by the wrong person.

Anchoring oneself usually begins by getting into a hypnotic trance (it can be done alone or with the help of a skilled practitioner). Once they are here, the hypnotist will ask them to recall a memory that induced a certain emotional state. Once they are in that state they will try to amplify that emotional state by getting them to recall as many sensory memories as they can. This is when they will help them to tie those feelings to a movement or gesture, etc. That chosen pose or gesture will be their anchor. Once this is complete, a person will be able to feel those emotions again by using that anchor when they need to.

If this calls back memories of Pavlov's experiment with conditioning dogs to certain stimuli, then you will be recalling right. This technique draws directly from the findings in that study, which becomes the reason it can be so dark. In the wrong hands, it can be used to train someone to change their feelings towards certain behaviors and adopt different ones.

Frame Control

This can be a simple to use tool that can be powerful during debates and negotiations. While it may have been touched on in earlier chapters, this will now be when the reader will come to a better understanding of how it works.

Controlling the frame is basically presenting an idea in a certain way. Controlling the frame in a conversation or thought pattern is referred to as reframing. An example of how this works is if someone gives you two choices. They are presenting the frame (the operative ideas) of the conversation. Since they presented it, they control it.

How would one then gain control of the frame? By reframing it. This can take the form of introducing a third option into the conversation (if we to stick to the previous example) that the other person will now have to consider. So the person who presents the frame controls it, but the other one can regain it by reframing it.

Dissociation

This is a visualization technique that can help someone overcome negative emotions during stressful situations. Psychopaths are often successful liars because they naturally disassociate their emotions from their actions, so they can be completely calm while lying, even when they know they've been caught.

Dissociation, for people who aren't that high in dark personality traits, will have to be done consciously as our brain's chemistry might often work against us when we most need it to be calm. A good example of how to practice this is to picture yourself outside of your body when facing a stressful situation. Observe the object of your stress and try switch your roles. Imagine what may be going through the mind of the person you want to seduce, or the boss you're trying to get to like you.

If one wanted to take dissociation a step further, they could turn around and observe themselves. Picture seeing oneself from outside the body and then act as if the body is acting completely separate from the mind and emotions. One can even go as far as to pretend they can control their body remotely while being outside it.

Mapping across

Mapping across is a tactic that falls somewhere between hypnosis and meditation. It can be done to one oneself or another person.

This technique involves using future visualization to make someone more likely to take certain action in the future under certain circumstances. It involves registering one's emotions about a certain event that will happen in the future and how they will want to react to it. After this, one can then consider how they feel about it deep down at that current point. The last step is to steadily replace the current feelings with the feelings one will want to feel in the possible world of that future even.

So if someone is afraid of something they have to do in the future, they can focus more on how they will feel once that event has taken place and passed. If they keep their focus on the feelings that will come after the event has passed, then their minds will learn to register those feelings rather than the negative ones they may currently feel towards it. By the time the event comes to pass, they will have been programmed (by themselves or others) to feel a certain way about the event which will increase the chances that they will do even better since they won't be going in with negative emotions.

Eliminating bad thoughts

Many people are usually held back from what they want because of negative thoughts that are the result of something that took place sometime in their past and has embedded itself into their subconscious minds.

There are three simple steps one can learn to use to prevent themselves from being overtaken by negative thoughts and act as they want rather than acting as their past dictates they act. The three techniques a person can use to do away with negative thoughts are:

Make bad thoughts intentional

While the natural intuition is to avoid thinking bad thoughts altogether, this may play against someone who is prone to neuroticism and other such negative thoughts.

By actively seeking out the bad thoughts and the memories that may automatically play out in one's head, you train your brain to recognize that you are actually the one who is in control of these thoughts. Over time, you will become desensitized to these negative thoughts. And the feelings attached to them.

Remember thought nature

When you catch yourself distracted by bad thoughts, it may be helpful to pause and observe the thought and its effects on you. When you've identified whether it helps or not, you can tell yourself 'it's just a thought' and dismiss it. Switch your mind to a more helpful or positive thought.

When you keep doing this, you realize that your mind is just a tool that you use and control, not the other way around.

Wash them out : Another method to help rid oneself of negative thoughts is to try to wash them out as they occur. Simply identify a negative thought you want to be free of. Make it as vivid and clear as you possibly can. Once you have, allow the colors to go a dull white and the volume to steadily fade.

Do this with the same thought over and over and you will find that it will become harder and harder to recall it at all.

Chapter6: How to defend from people with the dark side of personality: narcissism, sadism, etc...

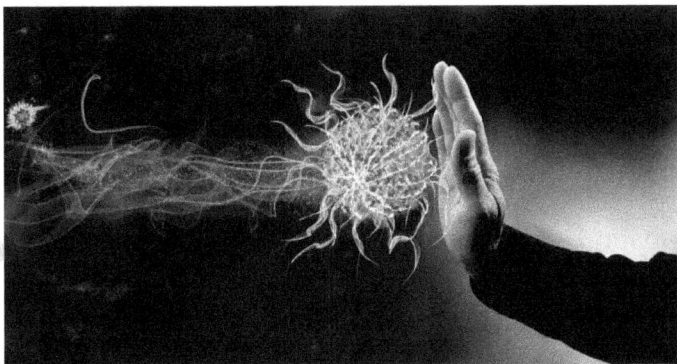

Narcissism

At its most basic, narcissism describes a sense of extreme entitlement, lack of empathy, and excessive admiration of oneself. The word comes from a Greek myth of Narcissus, where by a young man that was so handsome who apparently fell in love with himself by looking at his own reflection. He was callous and condescending towards those who loved him and drove some to commit suicide to prove their undying admiration of him. There are many signs an individual is narcissistic, and you have most likely met someone who displays this personality trait.

One of the most obvious signs of a narcissist is an excessive preoccupation with how they are perceived by others. They may spend an excessive amount of time grooming themselves and constantly presenting themselves in a light so positive that it treads on dishonest. The narcissist wants to be seen as a fabulous human being, constantly living it up and showing off their success and importance. They may exaggerate their achievements, social climb, or name drop about which important people they rub shoulders with.

In addition, a narcissist is an arrogant person who believes themselves to be more capable, important, and worthy than those around them. They are often exploitative and lacking in empathy, which means that they will use others to get what they want, with no mind that it may be hurtful to the victim. Narcissists are able to do this because they view others as extensions of themselves and are unable to fathom that others have priorities that are dissimilar to their own—no favor is too big to ask for, and the narcissist's self-centeredness makes them believe that they are justified in their actions. The narcissist believes his or her needs are above those of others—why shouldn't others be extra considerate of them.

Think you've seen anger? Just wait until you meet narcissistic rage. As explained in the above chapters Narcissistic anger or rage is the result of a narcissistic injury. A narcissistic injury afflicts a narcissistic person when their grandiose opinion of themselves is challenged or shown to be faulty. For example, a narcissistic injury can come from being rejected by a potential romantic partner or getting turned down from a job. Having this easily triggered response to rejection and disappointment frequently is the result of childhood trauma, such as a neglectful or abusive parent. The child, who senses that their parent does not love them, developed a grandiose persona in order to hide their deep feelings of inadequacy and shame, and to convince themselves that they will be invulnerable to such suffering at the hands of another ever again. Essentially, the narcissist is constantly trying to cover up how insecure they really feel by pretending they are the greatest, most fabulous and accomplished human being of all time.

Once the injury occurs, the narcissist may fly into what is known as the narcissistic rage. They will be unable to regulate their emotions and actions. The actions resulting from narcissistic rage can range anywhere from the silent treatment and temporarily withdrawing from others all the way to physical violence and serious abuse. Narcissistic rage occurs because the narcissistic injury is simply too much to bear. To the narcissist, it calls into question how great they actually and exposes them as imperfect beings.

There are many telltale signs of a narcissist and knowing some of their common behavior can make them easier to spot. For one thing, they will take credit for good things that happen to them, and blame bad outcomes on others, no matter what the reality of the situation is. If they get a bad grade on a project, they will insist that the professor has it out for them or that the grading process was unfair. If they have a good outcome, say someone of their preferred sex being friendly, they may insist this person was flirting with them. The narcissist wants to bend every story to present themselves in the most positive light and will not entertain any possibility that they may be wrong about something.

A narcissistic person is also obsessed with perfection. Not only do they hold themselves to high standards, which they often believe themselves to meet, but they also hold entities external to themselves to such a standard. The narcissist expects the people around them to behave perfectly, for events they attend to be perfect, and their circumstances to be perfect. They will become irate if they feel others have not met their expectations, even if they are unreasonable.

Another sign you may be dealing with a narcissist is that they speak in extremes about those around them. For example, they may profess how "special" you are and how much they love you one day, but as soon as you irritate them, they will disparage, insult, or neglect you. Despite a close relationship, a narcissist will always seem fairly uninterested in you as a person. You may tell them you had a bad day, or an interesting story about your day, and they will respond by talking about themselves. We have all had conversations like this—it's almost jarring. There you are, drinking coffee with a friend and believing both yours and your friend's needs hold equal weight in the conversation, when they suggest otherwise by talking about themselves nonstop. They will ask you a few questions about yourself and if they do, they seem to lose interest once you being to reply. In short, what's the biggest sign someone is a narcissist? A narcissist will make you wonder if their life motto is "It's all about me!"

Machiavellianism

Before we get into Machiavellianism, let us understand the word's namesake, Niccolò Machiavelli. Nicolò Machiavelli was an Italian statesman during the Italian renaissance during the fifteenth and sixteenth centuries. He was a diplomat, politician, secretary, philosopher, poet, historian, humanist and playwright. He is known today for his book, "Il Principe," or "The Prince." The book is a deep analysis of maintenance and possession of political power, written so Machiavelli could return to Italian politics from exile and hopefully be appointed a political advisory position by the Medici family. The book was so shocking at the time that Machiavelli was labelled and atheist. Machiavelli advocated for ruthless, cunning, and strategic methods of gaining and keeping political power. He is often credited with the saying, "the ends justify the means."

Given this introduction of Machiavelli the man, a deeper discussion of Machiavellianism as a member of the dark triad is appropriate. Machiavellianism includes low empathy, prioritizing power over others, strong ambition, and exploitation of others for personal gain. Machiavellianism is different from psychopathy because of the Machiavellian's emphasis on exploitation for personal gain, whereas a psychopath's very nature is insensitivity and callousness no matter what.

The Machiavellian believes human nature is inherently evil, and that deception is a justifiable way to attain goals and success. They generally undervalue human connection and overvalue wealth and power. The believe depending on others and cultivating meaningful emotional relationships is a worthless endeavor. When they manipulate or exploit others, they believe they have acted with reason and can justify their actions. They will do something terrible to complete a goal and when confronted, they will say, "Hey, I got the job done, right? It all worked out."

So, how do you know you're dealing with a Machiavellian? The Machiavellian is notoriously low on empathy; human connection always comes second to achievement and personal gain. To the Machiavellian, people are often conduits to other things—money, power, sex, or whatever else may seem worthwhile to achieve. Machiavellians are known to lie and exploit when necessary in order to get what they want.

Another common quality of Machiavellians is their penchant for strategy and calculation. A Machiavellian is good at sizing up others. They can read the room so to speak, and are perceptive of others' thoughts, feeling and weaknesses, despite the low empathy that accompanies Machiavellianism. Due to this calculating nature, these people tend to be patient. They are constantly collecting information and analyzing it to use to their best advantage. They know how to plan and wait for their rewards.

The demeanor of a Machiavellian often falls into one of two camps. They either seem aloof and emotionally distant or charming and friendly. Note that both of these demeanors may be present in the same person; someone may be charming and friendly but reveal so little about themselves that you may become suspicious or realize well into a relationship of any kind with the Machiavellian that you know little about them. This is deliberate, as the Machiavellian generally prefers not to share their true intentions with others.

With respect to their morals, Machiavellians are unlike psychopaths. While the psychopath simply lacks morals, the Machiavellian's are scattered, inconsistent, and ill-defined. The Machiavellian may claim to have certain ethical principles they value highly, but they are certainly willing to ignore them if they can justify doing so. Generally speaking, they have little respect for humanity as a whole. They think it is inherently evil, or at the very least not good, and are usually cynical.

Sadism

It's a bit of a given that most if not all people have sadistic thoughts, or have a little bit of a sadist in them. This does not, obviously, qualify everyone as a sadist, or even a latent sadist (even when given the right opportunity—as proven by psychologist Philip Zimbardo in his 1971 Stanford prison experiment, in which Stanford undergraduates took part as prisoners and guard in a mock prison, and soon proved that people are only too easily persuaded to inflict pain on others, and others are only too eager to submit to such authoritarian cruelty. It has been documented that we humans are naturally driven by instincts towards cruelty and aggression).

Nevertheless, humans aggress. Humans kill their own species—and often without reason or cause, and sometimes solely for pleasure. As far as cruelty goes, as it relates to Sadism, humans also appear to have a fascination with the spectacle of violence, either as participants or viewers. This fascination seems to transcend time and culture. Humans, not all but plenty, derive pleasure out of seeing others hurt. It could be argued that there's a potential Everyday Sadist lurking in all of us, but guilt, conscience, circumstance, context, whatever, keeps it tamped down. Or hidden.

Going by the conjectures, then the character of motivation to inflict struggling may actually be present in all humans, and the only major difference or contrast between the non-sadists and sadists narrows down to the latter group that has found the tactic to conquer their inward cruelty.

As to Everyday Sadist, a sadistic personality can center on many things. The will, as some researchers have said, maligning and humiliating, to practice absolute power with no restricted control or supervision over another, or the ecstasy brought up from other people's suffering. Sadists like to intentionally cause psychological pain, suffering or even sexual, purposely for their own benefits.

The enjoyment of the sadistic act can come via direct participation (core sadism) or not so directly, such as watching others inflict pain and suffering (vicarious sadism). The late American psychologist Theodore Millon proposed four types of sadism: explosive sadism, enforcing sadism, tyrannical sadism and spineless sadism,. The Everyday Sadist might have the traits of one or all four of these types, though each of these subtypes tend to stay within their personality traits. According to Millon's definition, the Spineless Sadist is insecure, cowardly, tend to swagger and brag, and picks out powerless scapegoats as targets. The Tyrannical Sadist loves to menace and brutalize others, hoping for their submission, cuts people down verbally, is accusatory and destructive, and tends to be surly, abusive, and inhumane; in a word: a bully, whether in person or online (internet trolls are largely Tyrannical Sadists). The Enforcing

109

Sadist are usually police officers, bossy supervisors, deans, judges, those who sublimate their hostility into the larger good, and therefore as public servants, profess the right to act harshly; they like to control and punish, and feel it their duty to ferret out rule breakers. The Explosive Sadist has a deep reservoir of bottled-up and often uncontrollable rage, and is prone to unpredictable and violent physical and verbal outbursts, only to later show contrition.

The Everyday Sadist can be any one of these Sadist subtypes. And true Sadists experience a kind of rush, repeatedly, whenever hurting others, and often, they lack the appropriate level of conscience needed to keep their addiction to sadistic pleasure under control.

Below are some of the more common outward traits of the typical Everyday Sadist.

They enjoy seeing people hurt and suffering. This could mean anything—from starting a rumor to publicly shaming someone, all just so they can watch that person squirm, and know that they caused that person their pain.

They enjoy hurting people. They enjoy bringing physical harm and pain to others. For example, this particular Sadist is standing in line at the movies. They don't like that the person behind them is standing too close, so they accidentally stomp on that person's foot.

They get excited by the idea of knowing others are in pain. A fight breaks out on the sidewalk. The Sadist doesn't shy away or call for help. They're right there, glued to the action. The violence, especially the suddenness of it, appeals to them.

They think it is acceptable to cause others' pain. Taking a kind of nihilistic, Hobbesian do or be done to approach to life, Sadists espouse a kind of affectless acceptance of kill or be killed. Hurt others before, or lest, they hurt you. Either way, they're OK with it.

They fantasize about hurting others. Sadists can drift off to thoughts of torture, mayhem, revenge fantasies, cruel sexual fantasies—all with a smile on their face.

They hurt others because they can. Squashing bugs seems OK. But when it's just for pleasure—that's sadistic. Similarly, Sadists think it's OK to bully others, and lately, they think it's especially OK to do it anonymously, online, where there are almost no consequences.

They like being humiliating others in order to keep them in line. If you're engaged in an argument with a Sadist, don't be surprised if they go from their inside voice to their outside voice in seconds—all the better to draw the attention of others and put you into an uncomfortable, embarrassing position.

Their sexual tendencies have an edge to them. If they want you to submit to sexual acts such as bondage, gagging, slapping, hair pulling, choking.

Conclusion

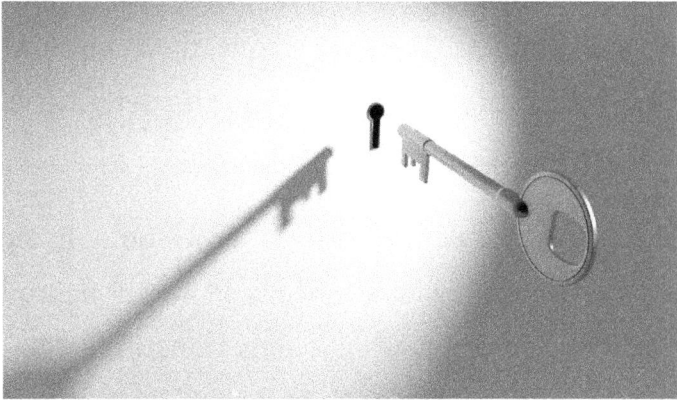

While many will assume they know the dark underbelly of humanity, they do not. They only learn what their own lives have conditioned them to see. They see what their individual histories may dictate they see. They often don't realize that they often see what others want them to see.

We all create an illusion about ourselves, our situations, maybe even our realities. We chose to live in them and portray them as true because it can often make life easier to bear. We do the things we do, not intending on hurting anyone around us.

In most cases, you will find that there is usually little to no malice in the words of most people in a civilized society. They go about their business doing the best that they can. Unfortunately, not all of humanity operates like this.

There are people in history, and some living among us today, who seemed have had a natural proclivity for doing what seems unnatural. They operate in ways that seem to baffle the minds of the rest of the population. They can even do things that can turn the stomachs of many decent people.

In order to help dispel some of the mysteries behind the ways of these people, you were shown how they can be a part of our everyday lives as lawyers, leaders, salesmen, public speakers, celebrities, etc. The essence of their very techniques was gutted and presented to you as honestly as possible.

On top of everything you had already learned about dark psychology, you were shown some of the other tactics dark persuaders may use against you in some unexpected settings. This all happened while a clear division between people who use this on purpose and by mistake was maintained as to avoid creating unnecessary suspicion and paranoia, especially in more sensitive readers. The journey would only get darker from there.

While you dove into the personality traits of these kinds of people, you were given a lot of insight into what makes people who can be considered as having 'dark personalities' tick. Hopefully, you have gained valuable knowledge regarding how these people may operate. Perhaps you even learned about the best ways to adopt some of these stratagems for your own benefit. How you use them is completely up to you.

One of the greatest tools in changing your own life for the better is learning to read people. Knowing the way other people communicate is a great way to improve one's own communication skills without saying a word. That is why it was imperative that you learn how you can read others because others are always reading you.

Bibliography/Sources

References

Derry McClean. Filtering on Psychological control and manipulation. Journal of psychology control and social beings.

Ken Wilber. Classification of different ways of coping with psychological manipulation. Forbidden psychology.

Edward Benedict. Techniques in dark psychology influencing humans and mind control.